JOHN UPDIKE was born in 1932, in Shillington, Pennsylvania. He attended the public
schools of that town, Harvard College, and the
Ruskin School of Drawing and Fine Art at
Oxford, where he spent a year on a Knox
Fellowship. From 1955 to 1957 he was a
member of the staff of the *New Yorker*, to
which he has contributed short stories, essays,
and poems. He has published many books,
among them five novels, *Couples*, *The Poorhouse
Fair*, *The Centaur*, *Of the Farm* and *Rabbit,
Run*; three volumes of short stories, *Pigeon
Feathers*, *The Same Door* and *The Music School*
(all published in Penguins); a children's book,
*The Magic Flute*; and three books of poetry,
*Hoping for a Hoopoe*, *Telephone Poles* and
*Midpoint*. His *Assorted Prose* is also available
in Penguins.

John Updike and his wife live in Ipswich,
Massachusetts, with their four children.

*John Updike*

# SEVENTY POEMS

*Penguin Books*

Penguin Books Ltd, Harmondsworth, Middlesex, England
Penguin Books Australia Ltd, Ringwood, Victoria, Australia

—

This selection is taken from *Telephone Poles*,
first published in the U.K. by André Deutsch in 1964,
and from *Midpoint*, first published in the U.K. by
André Deutsch in 1969
Published in Penguin Books 1972

—

Made and printed in Great Britain
by Richard Clay (The Chaucer Press) Ltd,
Bungay, Suffolk
Set in Monotype Ehrhardt

# Contents

5

# Acknowledgements

Some of these poems were previously published in the following magazines: *New Yorker*, *New Republic*, *Harper's Magazine*, *Atlantic Monthly*, *American Scholar*, *Look*, *Polemic*, *Première*, *Saturday Review*, *Transatlantic Review*, *Commonweal*, *Syracuse 10*, and *Christian Century*.

'Dog's Death' was first printed as a broadside sheet by The Adams House and Lowell House Printers at Harvard University. Canto III of 'Midpoint' is closely based upon the September 1967 issue of *Scientific American* and appeared in the January 1969 issue of that magazine. The Walt Whitman lines in Canto IV are all from 'Song of Myself'.

# Seagulls

A gull, up close,
looks surprisingly stuffed.
His fluffy chest seems filled
with an inexpensive taxidermist's material
rather lumpily inserted. The legs,
unbent, are childish crayon strokes –
too simple to be workable.
And even the feather-markings,
whose intricate symmetry is the usual glory of birds,
are in the gull slovenly,
as if God makes too many
to make them very well.

Are they intelligent?
We imagine so, because they are ugly.
The sardonic one-eyed profile, slightly cross,
the narrow, ectomorphic head, badly combed,
the wide and nervous and well-muscled rump
all suggest deskwork: shipping rates
by day, Schopenhauer
by night, and endless coffee.

At that hour on the beach
when the flies begin biting in the renewed coolness
and the backsliding skin of the after-surf
reflects a pink shimmer before being blotted,
the gulls stand around in the dimpled sand
like those melancholy European crowds
that gather in cobbled public squares in the wake

of assassinations and invasions,
heads cocked to hear the latest radio reports.

It is also this hour when plump young couples
walk down to the water, bumping together,
and stand thigh-deep in the rhythmic glass.
Then they walk back toward the car,
tugging as if at a secret between them,
but which neither quite knows;
walk capricious paths through the scattering gulls,
as in some mythologies
beautiful gods stroll unconcerned
among our mortal apprehensions.

## Upon Learning that
## a Bird Exists Called the Turnstone

A turnstone turned rover
And went through ten turnstiles,
Admiring the clover
And turnsole and fern styles.

The Turneresque landscape
She scanned for a lover;
She'd heard one good turnstone
Deserves another.

She took to the turnpike
And travelled to Dover,
Where turnips enjoy
A rapid turnover.

In vain did she hover
And earnestly burn
With yearning; above her
The terns cried, 'Return!'

# The High-Hearts

Assumption of erect posture in man lifts the heart higher
above the ground than in any other animal now living except the giraffe and the elephant.

– *From an article titled 'Anatomy' in*
Encyclopaedia Britannica

Proud elephant, by accident of bulk,
Upreared the mammoth cardiacal hulk
That plunged his storm of blood through canvas veins.
Enthroned beneath his tusks, unseen, it reigns
In dark state, stoutly ribbed, suffused with doubt,
Where lions have to leap to seek it out.

Herbivorous giraffe, in dappled love
With green and sunstruck edibles above,
Yearned with his bones; in an aeon or so,
His glad heart left his ankles far below,
And there, where forelegs turn to throat, it trem-
Bles like a blossom halfway up a stem.

Poor man, an ape, anxious to use his paws,
Became erect and held the pose because
His brain, developing beyond his ken,
Kept whispering, 'The universe wants men.'
So still he strains to keep his heart aloft,
Too high and low at once, too hard and soft.

## Earthworm

We pattern our Heaven
on bright butterflies,
but it must be that even
in earth Heaven lies.

The worm we uproot
in turning a spade
returns, careful brute,
to the peace he has made.

God blesses him; he
gives praise with his toil,
lends comfort to me,
and aërates the soil.

Immersed in the facts,
one must worship there;
claustrophobia attacks
us even in air.

# Telephone Poles

They have been with us a long time.
They will outlast the elms.
Our eyes, like the eyes of a savage sieving the trees
In his search for game,
Run through them. They blend along small-town streets
Like a race of giants that have faded into mere mythology.
Our eyes, washed clean of belief,
Lift incredulous to their fearsome crowns of bolts, trusses,
    struts, nuts, insulators, and such
Barnacles as compose
These weathered encrustations of electrical debris –
Each a Gorgon's head, which, seized right,
Could stun us to stone.

Yet they are ours. We made them.
See here, where the cleats of linemen
Have roughened a second bark
Onto the bald trunk. And these spikes
Have been driven sideways at intervals handy for human legs.
The Nature of our construction is in every way
A better fit than the Nature it displaces.
What other tree can you climb where the birds' twitter,
Unscrambled, is English? True, their thin shade is negligible,
But then again there is not that tragic autumnal
Casting-off of leaves to outface annually.
These giants are more constant than evergreens
By being never green.

## Wash

For seven days it rained that June;
A storm half out to sea kept turning around like a dog
   trying to settle himself on a rug;
We were the fleas that complained in his hair.

On the eighth day, before I had risen,
My neighbors' clothes had rushed into all the back yards
And lifted up their arms in praise.

From an upstairs window it seemed prehistorical:
Through the sheds and fences and vegetable gardens,
Workshirts and nightgowns, long-soaked in the cellar,

Underpants, striped towels, diapers, child's overalls,
Bibs and black bras thronging the sunshine
With hosannas of cotton and halleluiahs of wool.

## The Short Days

I like the way, in winter, cars
Ignite beneath the lingering stars
And, with a cough or two, unpark,
And roar to work still in the dark.

Like some great father, slugabed,
Whose children crack the dawn with play,
The sun retains a heavy head
Behind the hill, and stalls the day.

Then red rims gild the gutter-spouts;
The streetlamp pales; the milk-truck fades;
And housewives – husbands gone – wash doubts
Down sinks and raise the glowing shades.

The cars are gone, they will return
When headlights in a new night burn;
Between long drinks of Acheron
The thirst of broad day has begun.

## Maples in a Spruce Forest

They live by attenuation,
　Straining, vine-thin,
Up to gaps their gold leaves crowd
　Like drowning faces surfacing.

Wherever dappled sun persists,
　Shy leaves work photosynthesis;
Until I saw these slender doomed,
　I did not know what a maple is.

The life that plumps the oval
　In the open meadow full
Is beggared here, distended toward
　The dying light available.

Maturity of sullen spruce
　Will murder these deciduous;
A little while, the fretted gloom
　Is dappled with chartreuse.

# *Vermont*

Here green is king again,
Usurping honest men.
Like Brazilian cathedrals gone under to creepers,
Gray silos mourn their keepers.

Here ski tows
And shy cows
Alone pin the ragged slopes to the earth
Of profitable worth.

Hawks, professors,
And summering ministers
Roost on the mountainsides of poverty
And sniff the poetry,

And every year
The big black bear,
Slavering through the woods with scrolling mouth,
Comes further south.

# *Hoeing*

I sometimes fear the younger generation will be deprived
   of the pleasures of hoeing;
    there is no knowing
how many souls have been formed by this simple exercise.

The dry earth like a great scab breaks, revealing
   moist-dark loam –
    the pea-root's home,
a fertile wound perpetually healing.

How neatly the green weeds go under!
   The blade chops the earth new.
    Ignorant the wise boy who
has never performed this simple, stupid, and useful wonder.

## February 22

Three boys, American, in dungarees,
walk at a slant across the street
against the mild slant of the winter sun,
moseying out this small, still holiday.

The back of the cold is broken; later snows
will follow, mixed with rain, but today
the macadam is bare, the sun loops high,
and the trees are bathed in sweet grayness.

He was a perfect hero: a man of stone,
as colorless as a monument,
anonymous as Shakespeare. We know him
only as the author of his deeds.

There may have been a man: a surveyor,
a wencher, a temper, a stubborn farmer's mind;
but our legends seem impertinent
gaieties scratched upon his granite.

He gazes at us from our dollar bills
reproachfully, a strange green lady,
heavy-lidded, niggle-lipped, and wigged,
who served us better than we have deserved.

More than great successes, we love great failures.
Lincoln is Messiah; he, merely Caesar.
He suffered greatness like a curse.
He fathered our country, we feel, without great joy.

But let us love him now, for he crossed the famous ice,
brought us out of winter, stood, and surveyed
the breadth of our land exulting in the sun:
looked forward to the summer that is past.

## Movie House

View it, by day, from the back,
from the parking lot in the rear,
for from this angle only
the beautiful brick blankness can be grasped.
Monumentality
wears one face in all ages.

No windows intrude real light
into this temple of shades,
and the size of it,
the size of the great rear wall measures
the breadth of the dreams we have had here.
It dwarfs the village bank,
outlooms the town hall,
and even in its decline
makes the bright-ceilinged supermarket seem mean.

Stark closet of stealthy rapture,
vast introspective camera
wherein our most daring self-projections
were given familiar names:
stand, stand by your macadam lake
and tell the aeons of our extinction
that we too could house our gods,
could secrete a pyramid
to sight the stars by.

## The Stunt Flier

I come into my dim bedroom
innocently and my baby
is lying in her crib face-down;
just a hemisphere of the half-bald head
shows, and the bare feet, uncovered,
the small feet crossed at the ankles
like a dancer doing easily
a difficult step – or,
more exactly, like a cherub
planing through Heaven,
cruising at a middle altitude
through the cumulus of the tumbled covers,
which disclose the feet crossed
at the ankles *à la* small boys who,
exulting in their mastery of bicycles,
lift their hands from the handle bars
to demonstrate how easy gliding is.

## Mobile of Birds

There is something
in their planetary weave that is comforting.

The polycentric orbits, elliptical
with mutual motion,
random as nature, and yet, above all,
calculable, recall
those old Ptolemaic heavens small
enough for the Byzantine Trinity,
    Plato's Ideals,
     formal devotion,
seven levels of bliss, and numberless wheels
of omen, balanced occultly.

                    A small bird
at an arc's extremity
adequately weights
his larger mates'
compounded mass: absurd
but actual – there he floats!

Persisting through a doorway, shadow-casting light
     dissolves on the wall
     the mobile's threads
and turns its spatial conversation
dialectical. Silhouettes,
projections of identities,
merge and part and reunite
in shapely syntheses –
                an illusion,
for the birds on their perches of fine wire avoid collusion
and are twirled
alone in their suspenseful world.

## Les Saints Nouveaux

Proust, doing penance
in a cork-lined room,
numbered the petals
in the orchards of doom
and sighed through the vortex
of his own strained breath
the wonderfully abundant
perfume called Death.

Brancusi, an anchorite
among rough shapes,
blessed each with his eyes
until like grapes
they popped, releasing
kernels of motion
as patiently worked
as if by the ocean.

Cézanne, grave man,
pondered the scene
and saw it with passion
as orange and green,
and weighted his strokes
with days of decision,
and founded on apples
theologies of vision.

## Die Neuen Heiligen

Kierkegaard, a
cripple and a Dane,
disdained to marry;
the consequent strain
unsprung the whirling
gay knives of his wits,
which slashed the Ideal
and himself to bits.

Kafka, a lawyer
and citizen of Prague,
became consumptive
in the metaphysic fog
and, coughing with laughter,
lampooned the sad state
that judged its defendants
all guilty of Fate.

Karl Barth, more healthy,
and married, and Swiss,
lived longer, yet took
small comfort from this;
*Nein!* he cried, rooting
in utter despair
the Credo that Culture
left up in the air.

## Trees Eat Sunshine

It's the fact:
their broad leaves lap it up like milk
and turn it into twigs.

Fish eat fish.
Lamps eat light
and when their feast has starved their filament
go out.

So do we,
and all sweet creatures –
cats eating horses, horses grass, grass earth, earth water
except for the distant Man

who inhales the savor of souls –
let us all strive to resemble this giant!

# Fever

I have brought back a good message from the land of 102°:
God exists.
I had seriously doubted it before;
but the bedposts spoke of it with utmost confidence,
the threads in my blanket took it for granted,
the tree outside the window dismissed all complaints,
and I have not slept so justly for years.
It is hard, now, to convey
how emblematically appearances sat
upon the membranes of my consciousness;
but it is a truth long known,
that some secrets are hidden from health.

## Seven Stanzas at Easter

Make no mistake: if He rose at all
it was as His body;
if the cells' dissolution did not reverse, the molecules
    reknit, the amino acids rekindle,
the Church will fall.


It was not as the flowers,
each soft Spring recurrent;
it was not as His Spirit in the mouths and fuddled eyes of
    the eleven apostles;
it was as His flesh: ours.


The same hinged thumbs and toes,
the same valved heart
that – pierced – died, withered, paused, and then
    regathered out of enduring Might
new strength to enclose.


Let us not mock God with metaphor,
analogy, sidestepping, transcendence;
making of the event a parable, a sign painted in the faded
    credulity of earlier ages:
let us walk through the door.


The stone is rolled back, not papier-mâché,
not a stone in a story,
but the vast rock of materiality that in the slow grinding of
    time will eclipse for each of us
the wide light of day.

And if we will have an angel at the tomb,
make it a real angel,
weighty with Max Planck's quanta, vivid with hair, opaque
   in the dawn light, robed in real linen
spun on a definite loom.


Let us not seek to make it less monstrous,
for our own convenience, our own sense of beauty,
lest, awakened in one unthinkable hour, we are embarrassed
   by the miracle,
and crushed by remonstrance.

Written for a religious arts festival sponsored by the Clifton Lutheran
Church, of Marblehead, Mass.

## Vibration

The world vibrates, my sleepless nights
discovered. The air conditioner hummed;
I turned it off. The plumbing
in the next apartment sang;
I moved away, and found a town
whose factories shuddered as they worked
all night. The wires on the poles
outside my windows quivered in an ecstasy
stretched thin between horizons.
I went to where no wires were; and there,
as I lay still, a dragon tremor
seized my darkened body, gnawed
my heart, and murmured, *I am you.*

# Modigliani's Death Mask

FOGG MUSEUM, CAMBRIDGE

The shell of a doll's head,
It stares askew, lopsided in death,
With nervous lips, a dirty tan,
And no bigger than my hand.
Could the man have been that small?
Or is life, like rapid motion,
An enlarging illusion?
Ringed, Italianly, with ivy,
The mask makes an effect of litter,
Preserved inside its glass case like
An oddly favored grapefruit rind.

# Vow

(ON DISCOVERING ONESELF LISTED ON THE
BACK OF A CONCERT PROGRAM AS A 'MUSEUM
FRIEND OF EARLY MUSIC')

May I forever a Muse-
um Friend of Early Music be;
May I, no, never cease to thrill
When three-stringed rebecs thinly trill,
Or fail to have a lumpish throat
When crumhorns bleat their fuzzy note.
I'll often audit, with *ma femme*,
Duets of psaltery and shawm;
Cross-flutes of pre-Baroque design
Shall twit our eardrums as we dine,
And Slavic guslas will, forsooth,
In harsh conjunction with the crwth
(Which is a kind of Welsh vielle,
As all us Friends know very well),
Lull both of us to sleep. My love,
The keirnines (Irish harps) above
Tune diatonically, and lyres
Augment august celestial choirs
That plan to render, when we die,
'Lamento di Tristano' by
Anonymous. With holy din
Recorder angels will tune us in
When we have run our mortal race
From sopranino to contrabass.

## Agatha Christie and Beatrix Potter

Many-volumed authoresses
In capacious country dresses,
Full of cheerful art and nearly
Perfect craft, we love you dearly.

You know the hedgerow, stile, and barrow,
Have sniffed the cabbage, leek, and marrow,
Have heard the prim postmistress snicker,
And spied out murder in the vicar.

You've drawn the berry-beaded brambles
Where Mrs Tiggy-Winkle rambles,
And mapped the attics in the village
Where mice plot alibis and pillage.

God bless you, girls, for in these places
You give us cozy scares and chases
That end with innocence acquitted –
Except for Cotton-tail, who did it.

# Meditation on a News Item

Fidel Castro, who considers himself first in war and first in peace, was first in the Hemingway fishing tourney at Havana, Cuba. 'I am a novice at fishing,' said Fidel. 'You are a lucky novice,' replied Ernest.

– Life, *in June, 1960*

Yes, yes, and there is even a photograph,
of the two in profile, both bearded, both sharp-nosed,
both (though the one is not wearing a cap
and the other is not carrying a cat)
magnificently recognizable (do
you think that much-photographed faces grow
larger, more deeply themselves, like flowers
in sunlight?). A great cup sits between their chests.

*Life* does not seem to think it very strange.
It runs the shot cropped to four inches,
and the explanation is given in full above.
But to me it seems immeasurably strange: as strange
to me as if there were found,
in a Jacobean archive, an unquestionably authentic
woodcut showing Shakespeare
presenting the blue ribbon for Best Cake Baked
to Queen Elizabeth.

And even the dialogue: so perfect –
'You are a lucky novice.' Succinct,
wry, ominous, innocent: Nick Adams talking.
How did it happen? Did he,
convulsively departing from the exhausting regimen –
the rising at 6 a.m. to sharpen twelve pencils
with which to cut, as he stands at his bookcase,

34

269 or 312 or 451 more words into the paper
that will compose one of those many rumored books
that somehow never appear – did he abruptly exclaim,
'I must have a fishing tourney!'
and have posters painted and posted
in cabañas, cigar stores, and bordellos,
ERNEST HEMINGWAY FISHING COMPETITION,
just like that?

And did he receive, on one of those soft Havana mornings,
while the smoky-green Caribbean laps the wharf legs,
and the *señoritas* yawn behind grillwork,
and the black mailmen walk in khaki shorts,
an application blank stating CASTRO, Fidel?
*Occupation:* Dictator. *Address:*
Top Floor, Habana-Hilton Hotel (commandeered).
*Hobbies:* Ranting, U.S.-Baiting, Fishing (novice).

And was it honest? I mean, did Castro
wade down off the beach in hip boots
in a long cursing line of other contestants, Cubans,
cabdrivers, pimps, restaurant waiters, small landowners,
and make his cast, the bobbin singing,
and the great fish leap, with a splash
leap from the smoky-green waves,
and he, tugging, writhing, bring it in
and stand there, mopping the brow
of his somehow fragile, Apollonian profile
while the great man panted back and forth
plying his tape measure?

And at the award ceremony,
did their two so-different sorts of fame –
yet tangent on the point of beards and love of exploit –
create in the air one of those eccentric electronic
    disturbances

35

to which our younger physicists devote so much thought?
In the photograph, there is some sign of it:
they seem beatified, and resemble
two apostles by Dürer, possibly Peter and Paul.

My mind sinks down through the layers of strangeness:
I am as happy as if I had opened
a copy of 'Alice in Wonderland'
in which the heroine *does* win the croquet contest
administered by the Queen of Hearts.

## Bendix

This porthole overlooks a sea
Forever falling from the sky,
The water inextricably
Involved with buttons, suds, and dye.

Like bits of shrapnel, shards of foam
Fly heavenward; a bedsheet heaves,
A stocking wrestles with a comb,
And cotton angels wave their sleeves.

The boiling purgatorial tide
Revolves our dreary shorts and slips,
While Mother coolly bakes beside
Her little jugged apocalypse.

# Sonic Boom

I'm sitting in the living room,
When, up above, the Thump of Doom
Resounds. Relax. It's sonic boom.

The ceiling shudders at the clap,
The mirrors tilt, the rafters snap,
And Baby wakens from his nap.

'Hush, babe. Some pilot we equip,
Giving the speed of sound the slip,
Has cracked the air like a penny whip.'

Our world is far from frightening; I
No longer strain to read the sky
Where moving fingers (jet planes) fly.
Our world seems much too tame to die.

And if it does, with one more *pop*,
I shan't look up to see it drop.

# Toothache Man

The earth has been unkind to him.
  He lies in middle strata.
The time capsules about him brim
  With advertising matter.

His addled fossils tell a tale
  That lacks barbaric splendor;
His vertebrae are small and pale,
  His femora are slender.

It is his teeth – strange, cratered things –
  That name him. Some are hollow,
Like bowls, and hold gold offerings.
  The god may be Apollo.

Silver and gold. We think he thought
  His god, who was immortal,
Dwelt in his skull; hence, the devout
  Adorned the temple's portal.

Heraldic fists and spears and bells
  In all metallic colors
Invade the bone; their volume swells
  On backward through the molars.

This culture's meagre sediments
  Have come to light just lately.
We handle them with reverence.
  He must have suffered greatly.

# Cosmic Gall

Every second, hundreds of billions of these neutrinos pass
through each square inch of our bodies, coming from above
during the day and from below at night, when the sun is
shining on the other side of the earth!

– *From 'An Explanatory Statement on Elementary
Particle Physics', by M. A. Ruderman and
A.H. Rosenfeld, in* American Scientist

Neutrinos, they are very small.
   They have no charge and have no mass
And do not interact at all.
The earth is just a silly ball
   To them, through which they simply pass,
Like dustmaids down a drafty hall
   Or photons through a sheet of glass.
   They snub the most exquisite gas,
Ignore the most substantial wall,
   Cold-shoulder steel and sounding brass,
Insult the stallion in his stall,
   And, scorning barriers of class,
Infiltrate you and me! Like tall
And painless guillotines, they fall
   Down through our heads into the grass.
At night, they enter at Nepal
   And pierce the lover and his lass
From underneath the bed – you call
   It wonderful; I call it crass.

# In Praise of $(C_{10}H_9O_5)x$

I have now worn the same terylene tie every day for eighteen months.

– *From* Chemistry, *a Penguin book by Kenneth Hutton*

My tie is made of terylene;
   Eternally I wear it,
For time can never wither, stale,
   Shred, shrink, fray, fade, or tear it.
The storms of January fail
   To loosen it with bluster;
The rains of April fail to stain
   Its polyester lustre;
July's hot sun beats down in vain;
   October's frosts fall futilely;
December's snow can blow and blow –
   My tie remains acutely
Immutable! When I'm below,
   Dissolving in that halcyon
Retort, my carbohydrates shed
   From off my frame of calcium –
When I am, in lay language, dead,
   Across my crumbling sternum
Shall lie a spanking fresh cravat
   Unsullied *ad aeternum*,
A grave and solemn prospect that
   Makes light of our allotted
Three score and ten, for terylene
   Shall never be unknotted.

## *Exposure*

Please do not tell me there is no voodoo,
For, if so, how then do you
Explain that a photograph of a head
Always tells if the person is living or dead?

Always. I have never known it to fail.
There is something misted in the eyes, something pale,
If not in the lips, then in the hair –
It is hard to put your finger on, but there.

A kind of third dimension settles in:
A blur, a kiss of otherness, a milky film.
If, while you hold a snapshot of Aunt Flo,
Her real heart stops, you will know.

## Comp. Religion

It all begins with fear of *mana*.
  Next there comes the love of tribe.
Native dances, totems, ani-
  Mism and magicians thrive.

Culture grows more complicated.
  Spirits, chiefs in funny hats,
And suchlike spooks are sublimated
  Into gods and ziggurats.

Polyarmed and polyheaded,
  Gods proliferate until
Puristic-minded sages edit
  Their welter into one sweet Will.

This worshipped One grows so enlightened,
  Vast, and high He, in a blur,
Explodes; and men are left as frightened
  Of *mana* as they ever were.

## Marriage Counsel

WHY MARRY OGRE
JUST TO GET HUBBY?

*Headline in the*
**Boston Herald**

Why marry ogre
  Just to get hubby?
Has he a brogue, or
  Are his legs stubby?

Smokes he a stogie?
  Is he not sober?
Is he too logy
  And dull as a crowbar?

Tom, Dick, and Harry:
  Garrulous, greedy,
And grouchy. They vary
  From savage to seedy,

And, once wed, will parry
  To be set asunder.
O harpy, why marry
  Ogre? I wonder.

# Caligula's Dream

Insomnia was his worst torment. Three hours a night of fitful sleep was all that he ever got, and even then terrifying visions would haunt him – once, for instance, he dreamed that he had a conversation with the Mediterranean Sea.

– *Suetonius*

Of gold the bread on which he banqueted,
Where pimps in silk and pearls dissolved in wine
Were standard fare. The monster's marble head
Had many antic veins, being divine.
At war, he massed his men upon the beach
And bawled the coward's order, 'Gather shells!'
And stooped, in need of prisoners, to teach
The German tongue to prostituted Gauls.
Bald young, broad-browed and, for his era, tall,
In peace he proved incestuous and queer,
And spent long hours in the Capitol
Exchanging compliments with Jupiter;
He stalled his horse in ivory, and displayed
His wife undressed to friends, and liked to view
Eviscerations and the dance, and made
Poor whores supply imperial revenue.

Perhaps – to plead – the boy had heard how when
They took his noble father from the pyre
And found a section unconsumed, the men
Suspicioned: 'Poisoned hearts resist the fire.'
It was as water that his vision came,
At any rate – more murderous than he,
More wanton, uglier, of wider fame,
Unsleeping also, multi-sexed, the Sea.

45

It told him, 'Little Boots, you cannot sin
Enough; you speak a language, though you rave.
The actual things at home beneath my skin
Out-horrify the vilest hopes you have.
Ten-tentacled invertebrates embrace
And swap through thirsty ana livid seed
While craggy worms without a brain or face
Upon their own soft children blindly feed.
As huge as Persian palaces, blue whales
Grin fathoms down, and through their teeth are strained
A million lives a minute; each entails,
In death, a microscopic bit of pain.
Atrocity is truly emperor;
All things that thrive are slaves of cruel Creation.'

Caligula, his mouth a mass of fur,
Awoke, and toppled toward assassination.

# *Pompeii*

They lived, Pompeiians,
   as installments of flesh in slots of stone;
      they died in postures preserved,
by a ghoulish casting process, in the dank museum here.
   Outside the gates, living Pompeiian men
      peddle antique pornography.

   One feels this place
was cursed before that noon in 79
   when lunching gluttons found
their sturgeon mouths hot-stuffed with screaming ash.
   There is little to admire but the fact
      of preservation, and the plumbing.

   The plumbing lingers
like a sour aftertaste – the loving conduits,
   the phallic fountains, the three degrees,
so technically astute, of public bath. These Romans
   lorded a world of well-enslaved liquids; pornography
      became their monument.

## Roman Portrait Busts

Others in museums pass them by,
but I, I
am drawn like a maggot to meat
by their pupilless eyes
and their putrefying individuality.

They are, these Livias and Marcuses,
these pouting dead Octavias,
no two alike: never has art
so whorishly submitted
to the importunities of the real.

In good conscience one must admire
the drab lack of exaggeration,
the way each head,
crone's, consul's, or child's,
is neither bigger nor smaller than life.

Their eyes taste awful.
It is vile,
deliciously, to see them so
unsoftened by history, such
indigestible gristle.

# The Average Egyptian Faces Death

(BASED UPON AN ARTICLE IN *Life*)

Anubis, jackal-headed god
of mummification, will tenderly
eviscerate my corpse, oil it, salt it,
soothe it with unguent gods' tears and honey.

My soul will be a ba-bird,
a shadow, free to move in and out
of my muralled house,
though it's no pyramid.

In the court of Osiris the gods
will weigh my heart
for virtue; in the Field of Reeds
baboons worship Re,
and barley grows, and
beetle-headed Khepri, god of early morning,
kisses the misted canals.

Atum the creator has set
a smoky partition in the midst of things,
but the Nile flows through;
death has no other name than *ankh*, life.

## Seal in Nature

Seen from down the beach, the seal
seemed a polished piece of the rock he was on.
Closer approached, he became distinct
from the boat-shaped barnacled mineral mass,
twenty yards safe from shore, he had chosen
to be his pedestal – a living sculpture,
a Noguchi, an Arp, a Brancusi smoothed
from a flexible wood whose grain was hair,
whose gray was white in the abstract glisten,
and black where his curve demanded a shadow.

Sea his amphitheatre, the rippling mammal,
both water and stone, performed aloof wonders:
he wound the line of horizon on his nose,
and scratched his back with the top of his head,
and, twisting like a Möbius strip, addressed
the sky with a hollowing ululant howl
echoing empty epochs when,
in acres of basalt sown thick with steam,
spaced stars of life took antic shapes
and God was an undreamt dream.

# Tropical Beetles

Composed of horny, jagged blacks
   Yet quite unformidable,
They flip themselves upon their backs
   And die beneath the table.

The Temperate wasp, with pointed moan,
   Flies straightway to the apple;
But bugs inside the Tropic Zone
   With idle fancies grapple.

They hurl themselves past window sills
   And labor through a hundred
Ecstatic, crackling, whirring spills –
   For what, I've often wondered.

They seek the light – it stirs their stark,
   Ill-lit imaginations –
And win, when stepped on in the dark,
   Disgusted exclamations.

# B. W. I.

Under a priceless sun,
  Shanties and guava.
Beside an emerald sea,
  Lumps of lava.

On the white dirt road,
  A blind man tapping.
On dark Edwardian sofas,
  White men napping.

In half-caste twilight, heartfelt
  Songs to Jesus.
Across the arid land,
  Ocean breezes.
The sibilance of sadness
  Never ceases.

The empty cistern.
  The broken Victrola.
The rusted praise of
  Coca-Cola.

Old yellow table cloths,
  And tea, and hairy
Goats, and airmail
  Stationery.

Copies of *Punch* and *Ebony*.
  Few flowers.
Just the many-petalled sun above
  The endless hours.

# *Antigua*

The wind, transparent, cannot displace
  The vertical search of sun for skin.
The colonel's fine-veined florid face
  Has bloomed though sheltered deep within
His shining hat's mauve shade. His eyes
  Glare bluer than the coral-bleached
  Soft sea that feebly nags the beach
And hones its scimitar with sighs.

His wife, in modest half-undress,
  Swings thighs pinched red between the sea
  And sky, and smiles, serenely free
Of subcutaneous distress.
Above, sere cliffs attend their hike,
  And colored scraps give tattered hints
Of native life, and, higher, like
  A flaw in glass, an airplane glints.

## Azores

Great green ships
  themselves, they ride
at anchor forever;
  beneath the tide

huge roots of lava
  hold them fast
in mid-Atlantic
  to the past.

The tourists, thrilling
  from the deck,
hail shrilly pretty
  hillsides flecked

with cottages
  (confetti) and
sweet lozenges
  of chocolate (land).

They marvel at
  the dainty fields
and terraces
  hand-tilled to yield

the modest fruits
  of vines and trees
imported by
  the Portuguese:

a rural landscape
  set adrift
from centuries ago;
  the rift

enlarges.
   The ship proceeds.
Again the constant
   music feeds

an emptiness astern,
   Azores gone.
The void behind, the void
   ahead are one.

# Some Frenchmen

Monsieur Etienne de Silhouette*
   Was slim and uniformly black;
His profile was superb, and yet
   He vanished when he turned his back.

Humane and gaunt. precise and tall
   Was Docteur J. I. Guillotin;†
He had one tooth, diagonal
   And loose, which, when it fell, spelled *fin*.

André Marie Ampère,‡ a spark,
   Would visit other people's homes
And gobble volts until the dark
   Was lit by his resisting ohms.

Another type, Daguerre (Louis),§
   In silver salts would soak his head,
Expose himself to light, and be
   Developed just in time for bed.

* 1709–67
† 1738–1814
‡ 1775–1836
§ 1789–1851

# Farewell to the Shopping District of Antibes

Next week, alas, BOULANGERIE
Will bake *baguettes*, but not for me;
The windows will be filled, although
I'm gone, with brandy-laced *gâteaux*.

TABAC, impervious, will vend
Reynos to others who can spend
*Trois francs* (*moins dix centimes*) per pack –
Forget me not, *très cher* TABAC!

Grim BOIS & CHARBONS & MAZOUT
Will blacken someone else's suit,
And FLEURS will romance with the air
As if I never had been there.

ALIMENTATION won't grieve
As it continues, *sans* my leave,
To garland *oignons*, peddle *pommes*,
And stack *endives* till kingdom come.

*La mer* will wash up on the sand
*Les poissons morts* regardless, and
JOURNAUX will ask, though I'm away,
'UN AUTRE MARI POUR B.B.?'

## Summer : West Side

When on the coral-red steps of old brownstones
Puerto Rican boys, their white shirts luminous,
gather, and their laughter
conveys menace as far as Central Park West,

When the cheesecake shops on Broadway
keep open long into the dark,
and the Chinaman down in his hole of seven steps
leaves the door of his laundry ajar,
releasing a blue smell of starch,

When the indefatigable lines of parked cars
seem embedded in the tar,
and the swish of the cars on the Drive
seems urgently loud –

Then even the lapping of wavelets
on the boards of a barge on the Hudson
is audible,
and Downtown's foggy glow
fills your windows right up to the top.

And you walk in the mornings with your cool suit
sheathing the fresh tingle of your shower,
and the gratings idly steam,
and the damp path of the street-sweeper evaporates,

And – an oddly joyful sight –
the dentists' and chiropractors' white signs low
in the windows of the great ochre buildings on Eighty-
    sixth Street
seem slightly darkened
by one more night's deposit of vigil.

# 3 a.m.

By the brilliant ramp
of a ceaseless garage

the eye like a piece of newspaper
staring from a collage

records on a yellowing
gridwork of nerve

'policemen move on feet of glue,
sailors stick to the curb.'

# Erotic Epigrams

### I

The landscape of love
can only be seen
through a slim windowpane
one's own breath fogs.

### II

Iseult, to Tristan
(condemned to die),
is like a letter of reprieve
which is never delivered
but he knows has been dispatched.

### III

Hoping to fashion a mirror, the lover
doth polish the face of his beloved
until he produces a skull.

# *Flirt*

The flirt is an antelope of flame,
igniting the plain
wherever she hesitates.
She kisses my wrist, waits,
and watches the flush of pride
absurdly kindle my eyes.
She talks in riddles,
exposes her middle,
is hard and strange in my arms:
I love her. Her charms
are those of a fine old book with half-cut pages,
bound in warm plush at her white neck's nape.

## The Blessing

The room darkened, darkened until
our nakedness was a form of gray;
then the rain came bursting,
and we were sheltered, blessed,
upheld in a world of elements
that held us justified.
In all the love I had felt for you before,
in all that love,
there was no love
like that I felt when the rain began:
dim room, enveloping rush,
the slenderness of your throat,
the blessèd slenderness.

## The Great Scarf of Birds

Playing golf on Cape Ann in October,
I saw something to remember.

Ripe apples were caught like red fish in the nets
of their branches. The maples
were colored like apples,
part orange and red, part green.
The elms, already transparent trees,
seemed swaying vases full of sky. The sky
was dramatic with great straggling V's
of geese streaming south, mare's-tails above them.
Their trumpeting made us look up and around.
The course sloped into salt marshes,
and this seemed to cause the abundance of birds.

As if out of the Bible
or science fiction,
a cloud appeared, a cloud of dots
like iron filings which a magnet
underneath the paper undulates.
It dartingly darkened in spots,
paled, pulsed, compressed, distended, yet
held an identity firm: a flock
of starlings, as much one thing as a rock.
One will moved above the trees
the liquid and hesitant drift.

Come nearer, it became less marvellous,
more legible, and merely huge.
'I never saw so many birds!' my friend exlaimed.
We returned our eyes to the game.
Later, as Lot's wife must have done,

in a pause of walking, not thinking
of calling down a consequence,
I lazily looked around.

The rise of the fairway above us was tinted,
so evenly tinted I might not have noticed
but that at the rim of the delicate shadow
the starlings were thicker and outlined the flock
as an inkstain in drying pronounces its edges.
The gradual rise of green was vastly covered;
I had thought nothing in nature could be so broad but grass.

And as
I watched, one bird,
prompted by accident or will to lead,
ceased resting; and, lifting in a casual billow,
the flock ascended as a lady's scarf,
transparent, of gray, might be twitched
by one corner, drawn upward and then,
decided against, negligently tossed toward a chair:
the southward cloud withdrew into the air.

Long had it been since my heart
had been lifted as it was by the lifting of that great scarf.

## Winter Ocean

Many-maned scud-thumper, tub
of male whales, maker of worn wood, shrub-
ruster, sky-mocker, rave!
portly pusher of waves, wind-slave.

# My Children at the Dump

The day before divorce, I take my children
on this excursion;
they are enchanted by
a wonderland of discard where
every complicated star cries out
to be a momentary toy.

To me, too, the waste seems wonderful.
Sheer hills of television tubes, pale lakes
of excelsior, landslides
of perfectly carved carpentry-scarps,
sparkplugs like nuggets, cans iridescent
as peacock plumes, an entire lawnmower . . .
all pluck at my instinct to conserve.

I cannot. These things
were considered, and dismissed
for a reason. But my children
wander wondering among tummocks of junk
like stunted starvelings cruelly set free
at a heaped banquet of food too rich to eat.
I shout, 'Don't touch the broken glass!'

The distant metal delicately rusts.
The net effect is floral: a seaward wind
makes flags of cellophane and upright weeds.
The seagulls weep; my boys bring back
bent tractors, hoping what some other child
once played to death can be revived by them.

*No.* I say, 'No.' I came to add
my fragments to this universe of loss,

purging my house, ridding a life
no longer shared of remnants.
My daughter brings a naked armless doll,
still hopeful in its dirty weathered eyes,
and I can only tell her, 'Love it now.
Love it now, but we can't take it home'

# Report of Health

### I

I am alone tonight.
The wrong I have done you
sits like a sore beneath my thumb,
burns like a boil on my heart's left side.
I am unwell.

My viscera, long clenched in love of you,
have undergone a detested relaxation.

There is, within, a ghostly maze
of phantom tubes and nodules where
those citizens, our passions, flit; and here,
like sunlight passing from a pattern of streets,
I feel your bright love leaving.

### II

Another night. Today I am told,
dear friend, by another,
you seem happy and well.
Nothing could hurt me more.

How dare you be happy, you,
shaped so precisely for me,
my cup and my mirror –
how dare you disdain to betray
by some disarray of your hair,
my being torn from you?

I would rather believe
that you knew your friend would come to me,

and so seemed well –
'not a hair / out of place' –
like an actress blindly hurling a pose
into the fascinated darkness.

As for me, you are still the eyes of the air.
I travel from point to point in your presence.
Each unattended gesture hopes to catch your eye.


### III

I may not write again. My voice
goes nowhere. Dear friend,
don't let me heal. Don't
worry, I am well.
I am happy
to dwell in a world whose Hell I will:

the doorway hints at your ghost
and a tiger pounces on my heart;
the lilac bush is a devil
inviting me into your hair.

## Fellatio

It is beautiful to think
that each of these clean secretaries
at night, to please her lover, takes
a fountain into her mouth
and lets her insides, drenched in seed,
flower into landscapes:
meadows sprinkled with baby's breath,
hoarse twiggy woods, birds dipping, a multitude
of skies containing clouds, plowed earth stinking
of its upturned humus, and small farms each
with a silver silo.

## Washington

Diagonal white city dreamed by a Frenchman –
the *nouveau* republic's Senecan pretension
populated by a grid of blacks –
after midnight your taxi-laced streets
entertain noncommittal streetlight shadows
and the scurry of leaves that fall still green.

Site, for me, of a secret parliament
of which both sides agreed to concede
and left the issue suspended in brandy,
I think of you longingly, as a Yankee
longs for Lee, sorry to have won,
or as Ho Chi Minh mourns for Johnson.

My capital, my alabaster Pandemonium,
I rode your stunned streets with a groin
as light and docile as a baby's wrist,
guilt's senators laughing in my skull's cloakroom,
my hurried heart corrupt with peace,
with love of my country, of cunt, and of sleep.

## Subway Love

Negress serene though underground,
what weddings in northward Harlem
impressed upon you this cameo
stamp of stoic repose?
Beauty should never be bored
with being beautiful.

Stark lights shatter at our speed.
Couplings cluck, the darkness yells.
The child beside you sidles in
and out of sleep and I,
poor sooty white man scarcely visible,
try not to stare.

O loveliness blind to itself:
sockets thumbed from clay wherein
eyelids are petals of shadow,
cheekbones and jawbone whose carriage
is of a proud rider in velvet,
lips where eleven curves live.

Eurydice, come follow me,
my song is silent, listen:
*I'll hold your name in love so high*
*oceans of years will leave it dry;*
*mountains of time will not begin*
*to move a moment of your skin.*

The doors gape wide at Fifty-ninth.
The kiosk steps are black with blood.
I turn and find,
rebuked by light,
you gone, Negress serene,
tugged northward into night.

## Minority Report

My beloved land,
here I sit in London
   overlooking Regent's Park ⎫
   overlooking my new Citroën ⎬ both green,
exiled by success of sorts.
I listen to Mozart
  in my English suit and weep,
   remembering a Swedish film.
But it is you,
  really you I think of:
   your nothing streetcorners
   your ugly eateries
   your dear barbarities
   and vacant lots
(Br'er Rabbit demonstrated:
   freedom is made of brambles).
They say over here you are choking
  to death on your cities and slaves,
   but they have never smelled dry grass,
   smoked Kools in a drugstore,
   or pronounced a flat 'a', an honest 'r'.
Don't read your reviews,
  A ☆ M ☆ E ☆ R ☆ I ☆ C ☆ A:
you are the only land.

# Air Show

(HANSCOM FIELD, BEDFORD, MASS.)

In shapes that grow organic and bizarre
Our Air Force ramifies the forms of war.
The stubby bomber, dartlike fighter yield
To weirder beasts caught browsing on this field,
With wry truncated wings, anteater snouts,
And burnished bellies full of ins and outs.

Caressing curves of wind, the metal smiles
And beds the pilot down in sheets of dials.
Eggheaded, strapped, and sucking gas, he roars
To frozen heights all other life abhors,
Where, having left his dirty sound behind,
In pure blue he becomes pure will and mind.

These planes, articulate in every part,
Outdo the armor-forger's Tuscan art –
The rivets as unsparingly displayed
As pearls upon a chasuble's brocade,
The wiring bundled thick, like chordate brains,
The posing turbine balanced grain by grain,
The silver skin so stencilled it amounts
To an encyclical of do's and don't's.

Our dollars! Dumb, like muzhiks come from far
To gaze upon the trappings of a czar,
Their sweat turned into gems and cold faïence,
We marvel at our own extravagance:
No mogul's wasteful lust was half so wide
And deep as this democracy's quick pride.

# Topsfield Fair

Animals seem so sad to be themselves –
the turkey a turkey even to his wattle,
the rabbit with his pink, distinctly, eyes,
the prize steer humble in his stall.

What are they thinking, the pouter pigeons,
shaped like decadent ladies' hats,
jerking and staring in aisles of cages;
what does the mute meek monkey say?

Our hearts go out to them, then stop:
our fellows in mortality, like us
stiff-thrust into marvellous machines
tight-packed with chemical commands
to breathe, blink, feed, sniff, mate,
and, stuck like stamps in species, go out of date.

## The Origin of Laughter

(AFTER DESMOND MORRIS)

Hunched in the dark beneath his mother's heart,
The fetus sleeps and listens; dropped into light,
He seeks to lean his ear against the breast
Where the known rhythm holds its secret pace.

Slowly, slowly, through blizzards of dozing,
A face is gathered, starting with the eyes –
At first, quite any face; two painted dots
On cardboard stir a responsive smile. Soon
No face but one will serve: the mother's,
A mist, a cloud that clearly understands.

She teases him, pretends to let him drop.
He wants to cry but knows that she is good.
Out of this sudden mix, this terror rimmed
With necessary flesh, a laugh is born.

# The Naked Ape

(FOLLOWING, PERHAPS ALL TOO CLOSELY,
DESMOND MORRIS'S ANTHROPOLOGICAL REVELATIONS)

The dinosaur died, and small
   Insectivores (how gruesome!) crawled
From bush to tree, from bug to bud,
   From spider-diet to forest fruit and nut,
Developing bioptic vision and
    The grasping hand.

These perfect monkeys then were faced
   With shrinking groves; the challenged race,
De-Edenized by glacial whim,
   Sent forth from its arboreal cradle him
Who engineered himself to run
    With deer and lion –

The 'naked ape'. Why naked? Well,
   Upon those meaty plains, that *veldt*
Of prey, as pellmell they competed
   With cheetahs, hairy primates overheated;
Selection pressure, just though cruel,
    Favored the cool.

Unlikeliest of hunters, nude
   And weak and tardy to mature,
This ill-cast carnivore attacked,
   With weapons he invented, *in a pack*.
The tribe was born. To set men free,
    The family

Evolved; monogamy occurred.
   The female – sexually alert
Throughout the month, equipped to have
   Pronounced orgasms – perpetrated love.
The married state decreed its *lex*
   *Privata :* sex.

And Nature, pandering, bestowed
   On virgin ears erotic lobes
And hung on women hemispheres
   That imitate their once-attractive rears:
A social animal disarms
    With frontal charms.

All too erogenous, the ape
   To give his lusts a decent shape
Conceived the cocktail party where
   Unmates refuse to touch each other's hair
And make small 'grooming' talk instead
   Of going to bed.

He drowns his body scents in baths
   And if, in some conflux of paths,
He bumps another, says, 'Excuse
   Me, *please*.' He suffers rashes and subdues
Aggressiveness by making fists
    And laundry lists,

Suspension bridges, aeroplanes,
   And charts that show biweekly gains
And losses. Noble animal!
   To try to lead on this terrestrial ball,
With grasping hand and saucy wife,
    The upright life.

# In Extremis

I saw my toes the other day.
I hadn't looked at them for months.
Indeed, they might have passed away.
And yet they were my best friends once.

When I was small, I knew them well.
I counted on them up to ten
And put them in my mouth to tell
The larger from the lesser. Then

I loved them better than my ears,
My elbows, adenoids, and heart.
But with the swelling of the years
We drifted, toes and I, apart.

Now, gnarled and pale, each said, *j'accuse!* –
I hid them quickly in my shoes.

# *Home Movies*

How the children have changed! Rapt we stare
   At flickering lost Edens where
   Pale infants, squinting, seem to hark
To their older selves laughing in the dark.

And then, by the trellis in some old Spring –
   The seasons are unaltering –
   We gather, smoother and less bald,
Innocently clowning, having been called

By the cruelly invisible cameraman.
   How silently time ran!
   We cannot climb back, nor can our friends,
To that calm light. The brief film ends.

## Lamplight

Sent straight from suns
on slender stems
whose fangèd tendrils
leech the walls,
it sadly falls
on table tops
and barren floors
where rugs lie flat
as sunburnt crops.

Yet by this glow,
while daylight leans
outside the door
like an idle ax,
green voices wax,
red tongues thrust seeds
deep in the soil
of our harrowed needs,
and conversations grow.

# Décor

Brown dominates this bar
where men come to age:
the waiters Negro,
the whiskey unwatered,
the overheard voices from Texas,
the cigars and varnished wood.

Brown, the implication is,
is a shade of the soul,
the color of a man:
well-tanned and stained
to the innermost vein
as if life is a long curing.

## Dog's Death

She must have been kicked unseen or brushed by a car.
Too young to know much, she was beginning to learn
To use the newspapers spread on the kitchen floor
And to win, wetting there, the words, 'Good dog! Good dog!'

We thought her shy malaise was a shot reaction.
The autopsy disclosed a rupture in her liver.
As we teased her with play, blood was filling her skin
And her heart was learning to lie down forever.

Monday morning, as the children were noisily fed
And sent to school, she crawled beneath the youngest's bed.
We found her twisted and limp but still alive.
In the car to the vet's, on my lap, she tried

To bite my hand and died. I stroked her warm fur
And my wife called in a voice imperious with tears.
Though surrounded by love that would have upheld her,
Nevertheless she sank and, stiffening, disappeared.

Back home, we found that in the night her frame,
Drawing near to dissolution, had endured the shame
Of diarrhoea and had dragged across the floor
To a newspaper carelessly left there. *Good dog*.

## Dream Objects

Strangest is their reality,
their three-dimensional workmanship:
veined pebbles that have an underside,
maps one could have studied for minutes longer,
books we seem to read page after page.

If these are symbols cheaply coined
to buy the mind a momentary pardon,
whence this extravagance? Fine
as dandelion polls, they surface and explode
in the wind of the speed of our dreaming,

so that we awake with the sense
of having missed everything, tourists
hustled by bus through a land whose history
is our rich history, whose artifacts
were filed to perfection by beggars we fear.

## The Angels

They are above us all the time,
the good gentlemen, Mozart and Bach,
Scarlatti and Handel and Brahms,
lavishing measures of light down upon us,
telling us, over and over, there is a realm
above this plane of silent compromise.
They are around us everywhere, the old seers,
Matisse and Vermeer, Cézanne and Piero,
greeting us echoing in subway tunnels,
springing like winter flowers from postcards
Scotch-taped to white kitchen walls,
waiting larger than life in shadowy galleries
to whisper that edges of color
lie all about us innocent as grass.
They are behind us, beneath us,
the abysmal books, Shakespeare and Tolstoy,
the Bible and Proust and Cervantes,
burning in memory like leaky furnace doors,
minepits of honesty from which we escaped
with dilated suspicions. Love us, dead thrones,
sing us to sleep, awaken our eyes,
comfort with terror our mortal afternoons.

## Sunshine on Sandstone

Golden photon white on granulated red
   makes brown,
wall-broad in this instance,
   house-high:
splendiferous surface, the stucco
   worn bare
here and there, stones nicked, cracked,
   flecked, marked,
scored warmly, worn considerably, having
   wept rust,
borne whitewash, mortar, known weather,
   these spots
seem meditating irregularities:
   Lord's thoughts.

# Fireworks

These spasms and chrysanthemums of light
are like emotions
exploding under a curved night that corresponds
to the dark firmament within.

See, now, the libidinous flare,
spinning on its stick in vain resistance
to the upright ego and mortality's gravity;
behold, above, the sudden bloom,
turquoise, each tip a comet,
of pride – followed, after an empty bang,
by an ebbing amber galaxy, despair.

We feel our secrets bodied forth like flags
as wide as half the sky. Now
passions, polychrome and coruscating, crowd
one upon the other in a final fit,
a terminal display
that tilts the children's faces back in bleached dismay
and sparks an infant's crying in the grass.

They do not understand, the younger ones,
what thunderheads and nebulae,
what waterfalls and momentary roses fill
the world's one aging skull,
and are relieved when in a falling veil
the last awed outburst crumbles to reveal
the pattern on the playroom wall
of tame and stable stars.

# *Midpoint*

## I. INTRODUCTION

ARGUMENT: The poet begins, and describes his begin-
nings. Early intimations of wonder and dread. His family
on the Hill of Life *circa* 1942, and his own present un-
comfortable maturity. Refusing to take good advice, he
insists on the endurance of the irreducible.


Of nothing but me, me
– all wrong, all wrong –
as I cringe in the face of glory

I sing, lacking another song.
Proud mouths around me clack
that the livelong day is long

but the nip of night tugs back
my would-be celebrant brain
to the bricks of the moss-touched walk,

the sweet cold grass that had no name,
the arbor, and the wicker chair
turned cavernous beneath the tapping rain.

Plain wood and paint pressed back my stare.
Stiff cardboard apples crayoned to sell
(for nickels minted out of air)

from orange crates with still a citrus smell:
the thermometer: the broom:
this code of things contrived to tell

a timid God of a continuum
wherein he was enchanted.
Vengeful, he applied his sense of doom

with tricycle tires to coppery-red
anthills and, dizzy in his Heaven, grieved
his crushed Inferno of the dead.

A screen of color said, *You are alive.*
A skin of horror floated at my feet.
The corpses, comma-shaped, indicted, *If*

*a wheel from far above* (in summer heat,
loose thunders roamed the sky like untongued wagons)
*would turn, you'd lie squashed on the street.*

That bright side porch in Shillington:
under the sun, beneath grape leaves,
I feared myself an epiphenomenon.

The crucial question was, *Why am I me?*
In China boys were born as cherishing
of their small selves; in buried Greece

their swallowed spirits wink
like mica lost in marble.
Sickened by Space's waste, I tried to cling

to the thought of the indissoluble:
a point infinitely hard
was luminous in me, and cried *I will.*

I sought in middling textures part-
icles of iridescence, scintillae
in dullish surfaces; and pictured art

as descending, via pencil, into dry
exactitude. The beaded curtain
of Matter hid an understanding Eye.

Clint Shilling's drawing lessons: in
the sun he posed an egg on paper, and said
a rainbow ran along the shadow's rim –

the rainbow at the edge of the shadow of the egg.
My kindergarten eyes were sorely strained
to see it there. My still-soft head

began to ache, but docilely I feigned
the purple ghosts of green in clumsy wax:
thus was I early trained

and wonder, now, if Clint were orthodox.
He lived above a spikestone-studded wall
and honed his mustache like a tiny ax

and walked a brace of collies down our alley
in Pennsylvania dusk
beside his melodic wife, white-haired and tall.

O Philadelphia Avenue! My eyes lift up
from the furtive pencilled paper
and drown, are glad to drown, in a flood

of light, of trees and houses: our neighbors
live higher than we, in gaunt
two-family houses glaring toward our arbor.

Five-fingered leaves hold horsechestnuts.
The gutter runs with golden water
from Flickinger's iceplant. Telephone wires hunt

through the tree-crowns under orders
to find the wider world
the daily *Eagle* and the passing autos

keep hinting the existence of. And girls
stroll toward Lancaster Avenue and school
in the smoke of burning leaves, in the swirl

of snow, in the cruel
brilliance that follows, in the storm of buds that marries
earth to the iron sky and brings renewal

to the town so wide and fair from quarry
to trolley tracks, from Kenhorst to Mohnton,
from farmers' market to cemetery,

that a boy might feel himself point O
in optics, where plane ABCD –
a visual phenomenon –

converges and passes through to be
(inverted on the other side,
where film or retina receive it)

a kind of afterlife,
knife-lifted out of flux
and developed out of time:

the night sky, with a little luck,
was a camera back, the constellations
faint silver salts, and I the crux

of radii, the tip of two huge cones,
called Heaven and Earth,
that took their slant and spin from me alone.

I was that O, that white-hot nothing, yet
my hands, my penis, came also into view,
and as I grew I half unwilling learned

to seem a creature, to subdue
my giant solipsism to a common scale.
Reader, it is enchanting to share with you

the plight of love, the fate
of death, the need for food,
the privileges of ignorance, the ways

of traffic, competition, and remorse.
I look upon my wife, and marvel that
a woman, competent and good,

has shared my years; my children, protein-fat,
echo my eyes and my laugh: I am disarmed
to think that my body has mattered,

has been enrolled like a red-faced farm-
boy in the beautiful country club
of mankind's copulating swarm.

I did not expect it; humble
as a glow-worm, my boneless ego asked
only to witness, to serve as the hub

of a wheeling spectacle that would not pass.
My parents, my impression was,
had acted out all parts on my behalf;

their shouting and their silences
in the hissing bedroom dark
scorched the shadows; a ring of ashes

expanded with each smoldering remark
and left no underbrush of fuel
of passion for my intimidated spark.

My mother's father squeezed his Bible
sighing, and smoked five-cent cigars
behind the chickenhouse, exiling the smell.

His wife, bespectacled Granma,
beheaded the chickens
in their gritty wire yard

and had a style of choking during dinner;
she'd run to the porch, where one of us
would pound her on the back until her inner

conflict had resolved. Like me, she was nervous;
I had sympathetic stomach cramps.
We were, perhaps, too close,

the five of us. Our lamps
were dim, our carpets worn, the furniture
hodgepodge and venerable and damp.

And yet I never felt that we were poor.
Our property included several stray
cats, one walnut tree, a hundred yards or more

of privet hedge, and fresh ice every other day.
The brothers pressing to be born
were kept, despite their screams, offstage.

The fifth point of a star, I warmed
to my role, threw tantrums,
and catered to the others for applause.

How old was I when to amuse them
I drew the Hill of Life?
My grandfather, then seventy-some,

is near the bottom, beside
a Heavenly sunset, though twenty years
in fact would pass before he, ninety, died,

of eating an unwashed peach.
His wife, crippled but chipper, stepped
above him downward and, true, did not precede

him into that sunset, but snored and slept
six seasons more before her speechless spirit
into unresisted silence crept.

A gap, and then my father, Mr
Downdike of high-school hilarity,
strides manful down the inexplicably unslippery

pencil line. My mother is at the peak –
perhaps she was thirty-five –
and starting up the lonely upslope is me,

dear Chonny, maybe ten. Now on the downward side
behold me: my breath is short,
though my parents are still alive.

For conscientious climbing, God gave me these rewards:
fame with its bucket of unanswerable letters,
wealth with its worrisome market report,

rancid advice from my critical betters,
a drafty house, a voluptuous spouse,
and *quatre enfants* – none of them bed-wetters.

From *Time*'s grim cover, my fretful face peers out.
Ten thousand soggy mornings have warped my lids
and minced a crafty pulp of this my mouth;

and yet, incapable of being dimmed,
there harbors still inside me like the light
an anchored ketch displays, among my ribs,

a hopeful burning riding out the tide
that this strange universe employs
to strip itself of wreckage in the night.

'Take stock. Repent. The motion that destroys
creates elsewhere; the looping sun
sees no world twice.' False truths! I vouch for boys

impatient, inartistically, to get things done,
armored in speckled cardboard
and an untoward faith in the eye/I pun.

## 2. THE PHOTOGRAPHS

ARGUMENT: The pictures speak for themselves. A cycle of growth, mating, and birth. The coarse dots, calligraphic and abstract, become faces, with troubled expressions. Distance improves vision. Lost time sifts through these immutable old screens.

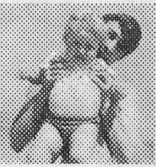

# 3. THE DANCE OF THE SOLIDS

ARGUMENT: In stanzas associated with allegory the actual atomic structure of solids unfolds. Metals, Ceramics, and Polymers. The conduction of heat, electricity, and light; non-symmetry and magnetism. Solidity emerges as intricate and giddy.

All things are Atoms: Earth and Water, Air
    And Fire, all, *Democritus* foretold.
    Swiss *Paracelsus*, in's alchemic lair,
    Saw Sulphur, Salt, and Mercury unfold
    Amid Millennial hopes of faking Gold.
    *Lavoisier* dethroned Phlogiston; then
    Molecular Analysis made bold
    Forays into the gases: Hydrogen
Stood naked in the dazzled sight of Learned Men.

The Solid State, however, kept its grains
    Of Microstructure coarsely veiled until
    *X-ray diffraction* pierced the Crystal Planes
    That roofed the giddy Dance, the taut Quadrille
    Where Silicon and Carbon Atoms will
    Link Valencies, four-figured, hand in hand
    With common Ions and Rare Earths to fill
    The lattices of Matter, Salt or Sand,
With tiny Excitations, quantitively grand.

The *Metals*, lustrous Monarchs of the Cave,
    Are ductile and conductive and opaque
    Because each Atom generously gave
    Its own Electrons to a mutual Stake,
    A Pool that acts as Bond. The Ions take
    The stacking shape of Spheres, and slip and flow
    When pressed or dented; thusly *Metals* make
    A better Paper Clip than a Window,
Are vulnerable to Shear, and, heated, brightly glow.

*Ceramic*, muddy Queen of Human Arts,
  First served as simple Stone. Feldspar supplied
  Crude Clay; and Rubies, Porcelain, and Quartz
  Came each to light. Aluminium Oxide
  Is typical – a Metal close-allied
  With Oxygen ionically; no free
  Electrons form a lubricating tide,
  Hence, Empresslike, *Ceramics* tend to be
Resistant, porous, brittle, and refractory.

Prince *Glass*, *Ceramic*'s son, though crystal-clear,
  Is no wise crystalline. The fond Voyeur
  And Narcissist alike devoutly peer
  Into Disorder, the Disorderer
  Being Covalent Bondings that prefer
  Prolonged Viscosity and spread loose nets
  Photons slip through. The average *Polymer*
  Enjoys a Glassy state, but cools, forgets
To slump, and clouds in closely patterned Minuets.

The *Polymers*, those giant Molecules,
  Like Starch and Polyoxymethylene,
  Flesh out, as protein Serfs and plastic Fools,
  This Kingdom with Life's Stuff. Our time has seen
  The synthesis of Polyisoprene
  And many cross-linked Helixes unknown
  To *Robert Hooke*; but each primordial Bean
  Knew Cellulose by heart. *Nature* alone
Of Collagen and Apatite compounded Bone.

What happens in these Lattices when *Heat*
  Transports Vibrations through a solid mass?
  $T = 3Nk$ is much too neat;
  A rigid Crystal's not a fluid Gas.
  *Debye* in 1912 proposed Elas-

Tic Waves called *phonons* that obey *Max Planck's*
$E = hv$. Though amorphous Glass,
   *Umklapp* Switchbacks, and Isotopes play pranks
Upon his Formulae, *Debye* deserves warm Thanks.


*Electroconductivity* depends
   On Free Electrons: in Germanium
   A touch of Arsenic liberates; in blends
   Like Nickel Oxide, *Ohms* thwart Current. From
   Pure Copper threads to wads of Chewing Gum
   Resistance varies hugely. Cold and Light
   As well as 'doping' modify the sum
   Of *Fermi* levels, Ion scatter, site
Proximity, and other Factors recondite.


Textbooks and Heaven only are Ideal;
   Solidity is an imperfect state.
   Within the cracked and dislocated Real
   *Nonstoichiometric crystals* dominate.
   Stray Atoms sully and precipitate;
   Strange holes, *excitons*, wander loose; because
   of Dangling Bonds, a chemical Substrate
   Corrodes and catalyzes – surface Flaws
Help Epitaxial Growth to fix adsorptive claws.


White Sunlight, *Newton* saw, is not so pure;
   A Spectrum bared the Rainbow to his view.
   Each Element absorbs its signature:
   Go add a negative Electron to
   Potassium Chloride; it turns deep blue,
   As Chromium incarnadines Sapphire.
   Wavelengths, absorbed, are reëmitted through
   Fluorescence, Phosphorescence, and the higher
Intensities that deadly *Laser Beams* require.

*Magnetic* Atoms, such as Iron, keep
    Unpaired Electrons in their middle shell,
    Each one a spinning Magnet that would leap
    The *Bloch* Walls whereat antiparallel
    Domains converge. Diffuse Material
Becomes *Magnetic* when another Field
    Aligns domains like Seaweed in a swell.
    How nicely microscopic forces yield,
In Units growing visible, the World we wield!

## 4. THE PLAY OF MEMORY

ARGUMENT: The poet remembers and addresses those he has loved. Certain equations emerge from the welter, in which Walt Whitman swims. Arrows urge us on. Imagery from Canto II returns, enlarged. Sonnet to his father. Conception as climax of pointillism theme.

At the foot of the playground slide

**FEET,**

striking the dust,
had worn a trough
that after a rain
became a puddle.

Last night
      lying listening to rain
               myriads of points of sound
                       myriads

memory of girl – worker for McCarthy – came to door – zoftig – lent her my wife's bathing suit – she pinned it – she was smaller than my wife – pinned it to fit – the house upstairs hushed – velvety sense of summer dust – she came down – we went to beach – talked politics lying on pebbles – her skin so pale – bra too big so the curve of her breast was revealed nearly to the nipple – 'If he ever got any real power it'd ruin him for me' – pebbles hurt her young skin – we came home – she took shower – should have offered to wash her back – passing me on way to the bathroom – skin – dawn-colored skin – eyes avoided – eye/I – I should have offered to wash her back – dressed in her own cool clothes she handed me back the bathing suit unpinned again – lovely skin of her arms untanned from a summer of campaigning by telephone – strange cool nerve taking a shower in married man's wifeless home – the velvety summer dust waiting to be stirred, to be loved, by the fan – left her by South Green – 'You'll be all right' – 'Oh sure' – girls hitchhike now – a silk-skinned harem drifting through this conscience-stricken nation

## CLEAN GENE

and empty arms

I made a note for this poem

in the dark

Where am I?

**ALL**

wrong, all wrong

myriads

window mullions

dust motes

Sense of Many Things

what was being said through them?

S o m e t h i n g

*'huh?'*

also we
used to
play hop-
scotch
with a
rubber heel ⟶

$$
\begin{array}{c}
\longrightarrow \qquad 1 \\[4pt]
2 \\[4pt]
3 \\[6pt]
4 \quad\; 5 \\[6pt]
6 \quad\; 7 \\[8pt]
8 \\[8pt]
9 \;{\scriptstyle\downarrow}\; 10 \qquad\qquad \textit{`Hey!'}
\end{array}
$$

You who used to swing on the pavilion rafters
      showing me your underpants
you with whom I came six times in one night
               back from St Thomas sunburned
in my haste to return
    my skin peeling from my chest like steamed wallpaper
my prick toward morning a battered miracle
         of response
and your good mouth wetter than any warm washrag
      and the walk afterwards toward the Park
          past Doubleday's packed with my books
your fucked-out insides airy in your smile
        and my manner a proud boy's
                   after some stunt
did you know you were showing me your underpants?
        did you know they said you laid
          beneath the pines by the poorhouse dam?
and in the Algonquin you
    in the persimmon nightie just down to your pussy

and your air of distraction
        your profile harassed against the anonymous wall
                that sudden stooping kiss
a butterfly on my glans
your head beat like a wing on the pillow
                your whimper in the car
you wiped blood from me with a Kleenex
        by the big abandoned barn I never drive past
                                without suffering
you who outran me at fox-in-the-morning
        whom I caught on the steps of the Fogg
                        the late games of Botticelli
you in your bed Ann in hers
        and the way we would walk to the window
                overlooking the bird sanctuary
our hands cool on each other's genitals
        have you forgotten?
we always exuded better sex than we had
        should I have offered to wash your back?
    you whose breast I soaped
                        and you my cock, and your cunt
indivisible from the lather and huge as a purse and the mirror
        giving us back ourselves
                I said look because we were so beautiful and
you said 'we're very ordinary'
        and in the Caribbean the night you knelt
to be taken from behind and we were entangled
                with the mosquito netting
and in the woods you let me hold your breasts
        your lipstick all flecked
the twigs dissolved in the sky above and I jerked off
        driving home alone onehanded
singing of you
    you who demurely clenched
your thighs and came and might have snapped my neck
you who nursed me

and fed me dreams of Manhattan in the cloudy living-room
and rubbed my sore chest with VapoRub
    and betrayed me with my father
        and laughed it off
and betrayed me with your husband
        and laughed it off
and betrayed me beneath the pines
        and never knew I thought I knew
your underpants were ghostly gray and now
    you wear them beneath your nightie
            and shy from my hug
      pubescent
      my daughter
who when I twirled you and would not stop bit my leg
    on West Thirteenth Street
you who lowered your bathing suit in the dunes
    your profile distracted against the sand
        your hips a table
    holding a single treat
your breasts hors d'oeuvres
you fed me tomatoes until I vomited
    because you wanted me to grow and you
said my writing was 'a waste' about 'terrible people'
    and tried to call me down from the tree
        for fear I'd fall
and sat outside nodding while I did toidy
    because I was afraid of ghosts
and said to me 'the great thing about us is
    you're sure of the things I'm unsure about and
    I'm sure of the things you're unsure about'
      and you blamed yourself for my colds
    and my skin and my gnawing panic to excel, you
    walked with me on Penn Street
      the day I tried to sell cartoons to Pomeroy's
and they took our picture

## LOANS

Oh Mother above
our heads it said

**LOANS**

I think of you and mirrors:
     the one that hung in the front hall
          murky and flyspecked and sideways
     and the little round one with which you
          conducted arcane examinations by the bedside
             I lying on the bed and not daring
look over the edge
     I was a child and as an infant
I had cracked this mirror in a tantrum
     it had a crack
     it was a crack
     O

**MIRRORS ARE VAGINAS**

and everywhere I go I plunge my gaze
    into this lustrous openness
       to see if I have grown
    Prodigal, you have given me love!
               Therefore I to you give love!'
'O I am wonderful!
        I cannot tell how my ankles bend'
'The smallest sprout shows
      there is really no death'

'And the pismire is equally perfect,
                  and a grain of sand,
                              and the egg of the wren'
'What is commonest, cheapest,
                  nearest, easiest, is Me'

Given **M** = **V**
and sex as a 'knowing';
      'knowing' = 'seeing'

∴ **PENISES ARE EYES**

'his eyes shut and a bird flying below us he was shy all the same
I liked him like that morning I made him blush a little when I
got over him that way when I unbuttoned him and took his out
and drew back the skin it had a kind of eye in it'

                                                    **Q.E.D.**

and you who sat
            and so beautifully listened
your gray hair limpid and tense like a forest pool
'nor whence the cause of my faintest wish'
            listened as I too effortlessly talked
                  after putting on my glasses
            (you called them my 'magic eyes')
shielding my genitals (remember
            the Cocteau movie where he slashes an egg?
not to mention poor Gloucester's
            'vile jelly')

talked but never explicit anent sex
       'shy all the same'
trying to wheedle your love
       and after months and years
you pronounced at last:
       'are demonstrations of flying ability to this ugly earth-
       mother figure, successively incarnated in the husbands,
       rather than true relationships with the women'
'Oh,'

I said, 'how sad if true'
       staggering out past the next patient
          in that room of old *Newsweeks*
             cured
sing                                           *oh*
    'adulterous offers made, acceptances,
             rejections with convex lips'
'Copulation is no more rank
           to me than death is'
'And mossy scabs of the worm fence,
          and heap'd stones, elder,
              mullen and poke-weed'
and Mother those three-way mirrors
       in Croll & Keck you
          buying me my year's jacket
my Joseph's coat
       I saw my appalling profile
and the bulge at the back of my head
       as if my brain were pregnant
'apart from the pulling and hauling stands what I am'
       I felt you saw me as a fountain spouting
gray pool unruffled as you listened to me
       telling cleverly how I loved the mail

how on Philadelphia Avenue I would lie
    in the hall with the flecked mirror
waiting for Mr Miller
      to plop the mail through the slot
          spilling over me

## MALE/MAIL

letter-slots are vaginas
    and stamps are semen swimming in the dark
        engraved with DNA
        'vile jelly'
    and mailboxes wait capaciously to be fucked
    throughout the town as I insomniac
        you pet
'To touch my person to some one else's
                is about as much as I can stand'
'And I know I am solid and sound'
           'The well-taken photographs –
but your wife or friend close and solid in your arms?'

'I tighten her all night to my thighs and lips'

the bed of two beds in the cabin
           whose levels did not meet
the pine needles myriad about us

and the double-decker bunk
        so that mounting me you bumped your
                              head
                              ↓
and the sleeping bag spread                  *ow*
on the lawn by the saltwater inlet
               mosquitoes
               myriads

  . . . . . . . . . . . . . . . . . .
. . . . . . . . . . . . . . . . . . . .
    . . . . . . . . . . . . . . . . . . . . . .
        . . . . . . . . . . . . . . . .

           scintillations of grass
           conversation of distant water
'The play of shine and shade
          on the trees as the supple boughs wag'
    What is pressing through?
           take me
'For every atom belonging to me,
          as good belongs to you'
*rien*
'And nothing, not God,
          is greater to one than one's self is'
*à trente et six ans*
'Behavior lawless as snow-flakes'
        having waited out numerous dead nights with listening
                    and with prayer
        having brought myself back from the dead with extra-
                 vagant motions of the mind
the slide
    the puddle
        the clack of box hockey
             the pavilion
many years later you
        sat on my lap at a class reunion
        your fanny was girdled and hard

a mother of four and I the father of four
        your body metallic with sex
and I was so happy I stuttered
perhaps Creation is a stutter of the Void
        (I could revise the universe if I just knew math)
I think it may all turn out to be an illusion
        the red shift merely travel fatigue
and distance losing its value like inflated currency
        (physicists are always so comfortably talking
        about infinite flashlight beams
        and men on frictionless roller skates)
and the atom a wrinkle that imagines itself
        and mass a factor of our own feebleness
'And to die is different from what any one supposed,
        and luckier'

        and if my body is history
        then my ego is Christ
        and no inversion is too great for me
        no fate too special
        a drowning man cannot pull
        himself out by his own hair (Barth)
and you above me in the bunk
        coming and crying, 'Fuck, John!'
        all our broken veins displayed
the honey of your coming a humming bird's tongue
        an involuntary coo

                    you pulled

*je pense que*
having inwardly revolved numerous Protestant elements – scree
    doors, worn Bibles, rubber condoms that snap and hur
    playground grass that feet have beaten into a dusty fuzz
    certain popsicle pleasures and hours of real reading, denta
    pain, the sociable rasp of Sunday drinks, the roses dozing
    the children bored –
        where you were always present

116

whose shampooed groin
               held all I wished to know –
   dance, words! –
I deduced
    a late bloomer but an early comer
    my works both green and overripe
(Proust spurred me to imitation,
        the cars aswish on Riverside Drive,
and Kierkegaard held back the dark waters, but)

*j'arrive à la pensée que*

$$\text{ASS} = \frac{\text{I}}{\text{ANGST}}$$

              you pulled me up

     I did fly
joy pulled a laugh from me
    your hands, voice fluttered
'Is that funny? Is it?'
    your nerves, voice tumbling
a two-body circus

                          *thank you*

the taint of performance

                          *forgive me*

↓ ↓ ↓ ↓ ↓ ↓ ↓ ↓ ↓ ↓ ↓ ↓ ↓ ↓ ↓

your
face

your
tense
hand

your
good
sad
shoes

'In vain the mastodon retreats
                  beneath its own powder'd bones'
these dreadful nights of dust
    of discrete and cretin thoughts
       the mind searching for a virtue
        whereon to pillow and be oblivious
'The palpable is in its place,
          and the impalpable is in its place'
rummaging amid old ecstasies
          'your poetry began to go to pot
when you took up fucking housewives'
    a hitching-post for the heart
       the devil rides in circles

# 1 2 3 4 6 7 9 8 01

*all wrong*

wherever we turn we find a curved steel wall
                of previous speculation

nd the water leaking from the main conduits
nd the gauges rising,
                              the needles shivering like whipped bitches
The nearest gnat is an explanation,
                        and a drop or motion of waves a key'
I effuse my flesh in eddies,
                              and drift in lacy jags'

*try again*

**FATHER,** as old as you when I was four,
I feel the restlessness of nearing death
But lack your manic passion to endure,
Your Stoic fortitude and Christian faith.
Remember, at the blackboard, factoring?
My life at midpoint seems a string of terms
In which an error clamps the hidden spring
Of resolution cancelling confirms.
Topheavy Dutchmen sundered from the sea,
Bewitched by money, believing in riddles
Syrian vagrants propagated, we
Incline to live by what the world belittles.
    God screws the lukewarm, slays the heart that faints,
    And saves His deepest silence for His saints.

I am a paper bag
                    I am trying to punch my way out of
Out of the dimness opposite equals advance –
                  always substance and increase,
                                    always sex'

'Always a knit of identity –
             always distinction –
                         always a breed of life'
you who breathes beside me
                    on Sparks Street spilled your cool nudity
across my eyes
                         above the summer dust
          body of ivory I have marred, silk I have stretched
you came against me kneeling
                    while a truck passed rumbling below
          and in Vermont
the only souls in a square mile of mountain                 garden
          the mantle lamps                                  is
          the deck of cards                                 river
          the Unitarian paperbacks                          flowing
          the spinning wheel gnawed by a porcupine          south
we too had our violence
'The butcher-boy puts off his killing clothes'
          beside me like a sacrifice
mildly curious as to the knife
          did conceive
                    in that square mile of wooded loneliness
a twinned point began to ravel
          you took me in
                    'the fish-eggs are in their place'
most gracious
                                                            *merc*

*'huh'*

# 5. CONCLUSION

ARGUMENT: The poet strives to conclude, but his aesthetic of dots prevents him. His heroes are catalogued. World politics: a long view. Intelligent hedonistic advice. Chilmark Pond in August. He appears to accept, reluctantly, his own advice.

An easy Humanism plagues the land;
I choose to take an otherworldly stand.
Reality transcends itself within;
Atomically, all writers must begin.
The Truth arrives as if by telegraph:
One dot; two dots; a silence; then a laugh.
The rules inhere, and will not be imposed
*Ab alto*, as most Liberals have supposed.
　　Praise *Kierkegaard*, who splintered *Hegel*'s creed
Upon the rock of Existential need;
Praise *Barth*, who told how saving Faith can flow
From Terror's oscillating Yes and No;
Praise *Henry Green*, whose lyric spirits sift
Through gestures, glances, shrugs, and silly drift.
Praise *Disney*, for dissolving *Goofy*'s stride
Into successive stills our eyes elide;
And *Jan Vermeer*, for salting humble bread
With dabs of light, as well as bricks and thread.
Praise IBM, that boils the brain's rich stores
Down to a few electric either/ors;
Praise Pointillism, Calculus, and all
That turn the world infinitesimal:
The midget of the alphabet is I;
The Infinite is littleness heaped high.
　　All wrong, all wrong – throughout phenomena
Flashes the sword of Universal Law;
Elegant formulations sever Chance

122

From Cause, and clumsy Matter learns to dance.
A magnet subdivides into Domains
Till ratios are reached where Stasis reigns.
An insect's structure limits it; an Ant
Can never swell to be an Elephant.
The Demi-urge expands up to a rim
Where calculable cold collapses Him.

  In human matters, too, Inductions act,
Cleave circumstance, and bare the general Fact.
*Karl Marx* and *Sigmund Freud* together show
Oppression alternates with Overthrow.
The proletarian Id combines its mass
With Superego's castellated class
To pinch the bourgeois Ego out of power:
The flag of Anarchy besports a flower;
The telescopic rifle and the cunt
Emblazon Urban Youth's united front.

  The world boils over; Ho and Mao and Che
Blood-red inaugurate a brighter day.
Apocalypse is in; mad Eros drives
The continents upon a shoal of lives.
Awash with wealth, the fair Republic creaks,
While boilermen below enlarge the leaks;
What child is this, who cherishes still more
Confetti on the tilting ballroom floor?


  Well, times are always desperate; this strange
Earth greets the old catastrophe of Change.
In bins of textbooks, holocausts lie stacked:
'No life was spared when Ghengis Khan attacked.'
It little counts in History's levelling eye
Just how we copulate, or how we die.
Six million Jews will join the Congolese
*King Leopold* of Belgium cleared like trees,
And Hiroshima's epoch-making flash
Will fade as did the hosts of *Gilgamesh*.

The Judgement Day seems nigh to every age;
But History blinks, and turns another page.
Our lovely green-clad mother spreads her legs –
Corrosive, hairy, rank – and, shameless, begs
For Pestilence to fuck her if he can,
For War to come, and come again, again.

   The meanwhile, let us live as islanders
Who pluck what fruit the lowered branch proffers.
Each passing moment masks a tender face;
Nothing has had to be, but is by Grace.
Attend to every sunset; greet the dawn
That combs with spears of shade the glistening lawn.
Enjoy the slanting morning, upright noon,
Declining day, and swollen leprous moon.
Observe the trees, those clouds of breathing leaf;
Their mass transcends the insect's pointed grief.
The forest holds a thousand deaths, yet lives;
The lawn accepts its coat of bone and gives
Next spring a sweeter, graver tone of green.
Gladly the maple seed spins down, between
Two roots extends a tendril, grips beneath
The soil, and suffers the mower's spinning teeth.
Nothing is poorly made; nothing is dull:
The Crabgrass thinks itself adorable.

   Cherish your work; take profit in the task:
Doing's the one reward a Man dare ask.
The Wood confides its secrets to the plane;
The dovetail fits, and reconfirms the grain.
The white-hot writhing Steel is tonged and plunged,
A-sizzle, into Form, all flecks expunged.
The Linotyper leans above his keys,
And feathers down a ton of journalese;
Engraver and Apprentice, in their room
Of acid baths and photophobic gloom,
Transform to metal dots ten shades of gray,
And herald Everyman's beginning day.

The Clergyman, beside the sighing bed,
Strains for a sign of credence from the dead.
The Lawyer eagle-eyed for Falsehood's glint,
The Doctor rapt for Angina's murmured hint,
The Biochemist analyzing sera,
The Astrophysicist alone with Lyra,
The Archaeologist with pick and brush,
The Nature-walker having spied a thrush –
Attentiveness! The pinpoint is the locus
Of Excellence in lands of softened focus.

    Applaud your Neighbor; admire his style
That grates upon you like a sawtooth file.
His trespasses resemble yours in kind;
He too is being crowded from behind.
Don't kill; or if you must, while killing, grieve.
Doubt not; that is, until you can't believe.
Don't covet Mrs X; or if you do,
Make sure, before you leap, she covets you.

    Like meat upon the table, we will spoil:
Time is the troubled water; Faith, the oil.
The curse of Tempo regulates the dance;
To move necessitates Impermanence.
So flow, flow outward; *Heraclitus* saw,
In Nature's crystalline, the fluid flaw:
Our Guilt inheres in sheer Existing, so
Forgive yourself your death, and freely flow.

    Transcendent Goodness makes elastic claims;
The merciful Creator hid His Aims.
Beware false Gods: the Infallible Man,
The flawless formula, the Five-Year Plan.
Abjure bandwagons; be shy of machines,
Charisma, ends that justify the means,
And oaths that bind the postulant to kill
His own self-love and independent Will.
A Mussolini leads to Hitler; hate
Apostles of the all-inclusive State.

Half-measures are most human; Compromise,
Inglorious and gray, placates the Wise.
By mechanistic hopes is Mankind vexed;
The Book of Life is margin more than text.
Ecclesiastes and our glands agree:
A time for love, for work, for sleep, for tea.
Organic music scores our ancient nerves:
Hark to its rhythm, conform to its curves.

All wrong? Advice, however sound, depends
Upon a meliorism Truth upends;
A certain Sinkingness resides in things.
The restless heart rejects what Fortune brings;
The Ego, too athletic, grows perverse
And muscle-builds by choosing worse and worse.
Our bones are prison-bars, our flesh is cells:
Where Suicide invites, Death-wish impels.
Earthquakes, Diseases, Floods, Eruptions, Drought,
Black Comets, Starry Landslides, Wreck and Rout –
Beneath a cliff of vast Indifference
We light our frail fires, peg our poor tents.
The sleepless mouse-gray hours gnaw and stress:
'The Wisdom of the Earth is Foolishness.'

Yet morning here, by Chilmark Pond, is fair.
The water scintillates against the air,
The grassy earth spins seed from solar rage,
And patiently denies its awful age.
I am another world, no doubt; no doubt
We come into this World from well without.
The seasons lessen; Summer's touch betrays
A tired haste, a cool autumnal trace.
The playground dust was richer, once, than loam,
And green, green as Eden, the slow path home;
No snows have been as deep as those my sled
Caressed to ice before I went to bed.

Perhaps Senility will give me back
The primitive rapport I lately lack.
    Adulthood has its comforts: these entail
Sermons and sex and receipt of the mail,
Elimination's homely paean, dreams'
Mad gaiety, avoidance of extremes,
The friendship of children, the trust of banks,
Thoracic pangs, a stiffness in the shanks,
Foretastes of death, the aftertaste of sin,
In winter, Whiskey, and in summer, Gin.
    The marsh gives way to Pond, to dunes, to Sea;
Cicadas call it good, and I agree.
At midpoint, center of a Hemisphere
Too blue for words, I've grown to love it here.
Earth wants me, it shall have me, yet not yet;
Some task remains, whose weight I can't forget,
Some package, anciently addressed, of praise,
That keeps me knocking on the doors of days.
    The time is gone, when *Pope* could ladle Wit
In couplet droplets, and decanter it.
*Wordsworth*'s sweet brooding, *Milton*'s pride,
And *Tennyson*'s unease have all been tried;
*Fin-de-siècle* sickliness became
High-stepping Modernism, then went lame.
Art offers now, not cunning and exile,
But blank explosions and a hostile smile.
    Deepest in the thicket, thorns spell a word.
Born laughing, I've believed in the Absurd,
Which brought me this far; henceforth, if I can,
I must impersonate a serious man.

*April–August 1968*

127

# John Updike

### COUPLES

A searching and poetic treatment of the involvements and aberrations of ten New England couples which exposes the life of a community with astonishing particularity.

### RABBIT, RUN

Stuck with an alcoholic wife, a child, and a futile job in a banal town, 'Rabbit' Angstrom finds that his powers of indecision are unlimited. 'A small-town tragedy . . . convincing, vivid, and awful' – *The Times Literary Supplement*

### CENTAUR

The atmosphere of an American small town is brilliantly evoked in this account of three days of crisis in the lives of George Caldwell, a clumsily affectionate father, and Peter, his artistic fifteen-year-old son.

### ASSORTED PROSE

These brilliantly perceptive reviews and autobiographical essays combine charm and wit with honesty and exactness.

*Three collections of short stories are also available:*

### THE MUSIC SCHOOL
### THE SAME DOOR
### PIGEON FEATHERS AND OTHER STORIES

*Not for sale in the U.S.A. or Canada*